THROUGH THE EYES OF
OPHELIA:
A STORY OF ADDICTION

THROUGH THE EYES OF
OPHELIA:
A STORY OF ADDICTION

Principal Roll, Staff
and students teach
one another of the danger
of drugs. God Bless...

David

David Butler

To order additional copies of this book, contact:
Xlibris Corporation
1-888-795-4274
www.Xlibris.com
Orders@Xlibris.com
115133

Table Of Contents

Introduction

Drug addiction is a terrifying, despair filled circumstance, and something I didn't think that I would ever experience. It is a killer of dreams as well as happiness. The first time I tried any drug, be it marijuana, cocaine, or crack, I was instantly addicted even though I didn't realize it. By the time I did realize, it was too late, and I couldn't control it anymore. Even though it was affecting my health, occupation, and relationships with the ones that I loved and cared most about, I couldn't stop. Nothing mattered to me anymore, and all I wanted to do was keep using. The following is a true story about my addiction to drugs, and how they destroyed my life and the things I loved most.

Chapter 1

South Of The Border

It was the summer of 2004. I had just gotten back from a month vacation in Puerto Vallarta, Mexico. Ah Vallarta how my heart longs for thee. Being a teacher at the time, I had summers off, so I enjoyed traveling. That particular trip to Vallarta was wonderful like always, but the drug use was less satisfying. Marijuana and cocaine were the drugs used that trip, but in reality I really wanted to smoke crack-cocaine. The isolation and paranoia were starting to engulf me. The euphoria experienced during the beginning stages of drug use was diminishing. Even though euphoria was turning to misery, I couldn't stop. My own personal hell had just begun. Not knowing what was happening, and still thinking I was in control, the disease of addiction had its claws in me.

I arrived back in Mesa, Arizona around the 4th of July. I moved into a hotel turned into apartments. Not the best place for an addict to live, but on a teachers salary, the price was right. All of the apartments had that same musty odor, the smell you would associate with that type of complex. A place where the seedy live, and the riff raff come out at night. Turns out it was just the right place for an addict to live or in hindsight probably not. Not understanding addiction totally, and not realizing I was a drug addict, I still knew I could find the drugs that I so craved.

My first encounter with crack-cocaine was in the fall of 2002. I was teaching math at Borman middle school, a school that was part of the Cartwright District located in Phoenix, Arizona. Soon after the year started I found out my dad was diagnosed with prostate cancer. I was quite devastated by the news as any son would be. The Cartwright District was a year round school, so after thinking about the situation I decided to resign from my teaching position, and go back to Iowa and help my ailing dad at the end of the first quarter in early October. It turned out he didn't want me to come home after all. I'm not really sure why, just pride I guess, but it would've been a great bonding moment for the two of us. Connecting with him in a special way is something I've longed for my whole life. Since I wasn't needed in Waukon I decided to flee to Mexico to escape from my problems, and feelings of inadequacies. Although, it was difficult to leave Ophelia, my beloved calico cat.

I had met a girl the summer of '02 when I was vacationing there once again. Her name was Patricia, a beautiful Mexican senorita. We had been corresponding, and it turned out she was going to be at her family's condo in October. A beautiful condo at the Bay View Grand located in the Marina. This was some complex, ocean front with a pool that had to be close to 100 yards long when all said and done. I spent days laying out by the pool and smoking weed, and nights drinking tequila and dancing at the Zoo bar. I'd do anything not to think about the pain my dad was going through, and my feelings of being an inadequate son. Patricia didn't do drugs and had no idea I was using. Like all addicts, I developed the skills of sneakiness and deception. I learned how to keep the disease of addiction hidden from the ones I loved and respected. Sure, because I needed to use, but also because of the shame and guilt I felt.

I kept in touch with my dad throughout my stay using a Mexican phone card, and the pay phone on the street outside the condo. It was a little bit worse for wear, but the reception was really quite good. The first time we spoke was the usual conversation. You know, I said,"How are you?" He would reply, "Fine." Then I said, "Are you feeling OK?" He said, "Yes." Once again not much said, just the peachy, cream scenario. When I called him the second week, the cream was gone, and the peaches were no where to be found. Once he spoke I knew something was wrong. The treatments for this form of cancer and all others must be horrendous. That's why I wanted to go home, so I could be there to support him. That day the treatment involved a catheter, so it must have been extremely painful. After that conversation I knew I shouldn't have honored my dad's wishes like the Good Book says, and gone back to Iowa to support him. I'm happy to say that after that conversation the news was much better, and to this day he is in remission.

Chapter 2

Hurricane Kenna

Hurricane season lasts until November 30, so there is always a chance that a hurricane could form off the coast of southern Mexico in October, and that is exactly what happened. During the third week is when the hurricane hit. Hailing from a small town in Iowa there is not much of a chance to witness a category 5 hurricane. Before the hurricane arrived it seemed surreal, beautiful days kicking it by the pool, and looking at what seemed like diamonds sparkling in the Pacific Ocean. As October 25th approached, and it was definite that hurricane Kenna was heading towards Vallarta, the preparation grew more intense. Until you experience one, it seems like a bit of a party. I was in Puerto Vallarta, my dad was dealing with cancer, I felt I just let him down again, and a category 5 hurricane was heading directly for us. Party like it's 1999, right?

The days leading up to Kenna's arrival grew more intense. There was greater anticipation of what was about to happen, but in reality, we had no idea on what was in store for us. Squalls were passing through that produced thunderstorm conditions, something I'm used to being from the Hawkeye state. It all seemed to be pretty common to me, so no big thing. The evening before Kenna hit, the storms brewing off the southern coast, over the mountains were becoming more ominous. It got so bad that the pirate ship that took tourists on the sunset dinner cruise had to stay in the Bahia de Banderas(Banderas Bay). The ship started to head out farther into the Pacific Ocean, but soon turned back to calm everyone's fears. The situation was a bit tense.

When we arrived back at the condo, the first thing we did was turn on the TV to check out the latest on Kenna. I followed along as well as I could since my Spanish is somewhat lacking. Patricia did the best that she could to translate for me. It's always interesting to check out another country's programming, because of the new learning experience. The station was showing a satellite picture of Kenna, it had a perfect eye wall, and was approximately 150 miles or 90 kilometers southwest of Vallarta. There was the standard category 5 hurricane view we've all seen on CNN, and it was a monster. As we were watching the update, all of a sudden the picture turned to snow. I looked at Patricia with amazement as she did with me. That's when I knew that by the time morning came around, we we're going to witness something like we never had before.

When we woke up the next morning we immediately rushed to the balcony's sliding glass doors, and took a look out at the ocean. We were experiencing hurricane conditions. The sky was gray and the ocean was rumbling. The oceans surge was crashing through the tiki huts turning them into drift wood. The ocean was rising, but the 15 foot sea wall was keeping the ocean out of the property for the time being. At the full force of Kenna, the surge was so great that the ocean rose higher than the the wall, came on to the property, and proceeded to fill the 100 yard pool with around 6 feet of sand. The surge also brought the tiki hut wood and huge sea boulders with it, resulting in the destruction of some of the first and second floor condo's. Amidst all the destruction, it was fortunate for Vallarta that Kenna's center made land fall about 30 miles north, which is about 50 kilometers, or the damage would have been much worse, even though it was extensive. The excitement and anticipation that I had felt before was replaced with despair and sorrow, and the dreadful feeling that I never wanted to experience something like that again.

The devastation at the the Bay View Grand was only the beginning. The city of Puerto Vallarta sits behind the middle of Banderas Bay, nestled in the mountains. It is an utterly magical city filled with many Mexican shops, the merchants selling indigenous items such as silver jewelry and other souvenirs. The street heading into the city, Paseo Diaz Ordaz, was lined with large metal pristine sculptures depicting the Mexican culture. Once again there's a sea wall protecting the city, and if my recollection is correct, it was at least 20 feet high. The surge was so great that the ocean rose above the 20 foot sea wall, and tremendous waves crashed into many of those shops taking a great deal of jewelry and other souvenirs out to sea never to be seen again. Many of the large sculptures were damaged as well. A fairly good sized yacht was washed up about 3 blocks into the city. Numerous homes and resorts along the coast were also damaged, if not destroyed. Many of the locals had incredible stories of waves as high as 90 feet rolling over La Playa de Los Muertos(the beach of the dead), and subsequently into the downtown shops. Looting did occur, but the Mexican military soon took care of that and restored order. You know you're in a different country when there are young men, probably in their late teens or early twenties, dressed in green military pants and white t-shirts riding around in the back of fully fledged large trucks, and armed with AK-47's.

Chapter 3

Stay Or Go?

The last couple of weeks with Patricia were spent watching the Mexican laborers clean up the property, and checking out the clean-up effort in the city. There's a lot of prejudice on all sides when it comes to Mexico, but if those that are could have witnessed what I did, their walls of hatred just might have been penetrated. The temperature in Vallarta at that time of year is still in the low to mid 80's with high humidity. Well, these guys shoveled by hand, approximately 45,000 cubic feet of sand in the hot, sweltering Vallarta sun. Keep in mind there were no machines being used, except the human body. A couple of workers would start shoveling, continue to the point of collapsing, and then would hand the shovels over to the next guys while they would catch their breath. This was a dawn to dusk project, and after a week of sweat and tears they had a section of the pool ready for use again. There were 3 sections to the pool that measured about 300 feet by 25 feet, and 6 feet deep.

Pretty hard work for 100 pesos per day, which was about $10 a day U.S at the time.

Patricia had rented out the family condo for the month of November, so I had a decision to make. Do I go to Cuenavaca with her and meet her family, or stay in Vallarta and attempt to sell timeshares at one of the resorts. After deliberating a couple of days, I decided to stay in Vallarta and give the timeshare thing a shot. Although in reality the drugs wouldn't let me go. It would've been interesting to see and learn more about the Mexican culture, but my reasons for staying was to try to make some big money to help my ailing dad and to keep abusing drugs. I was hoping to make make enough money to pay off his mortgage, so that a retired postman driving a school bus to make ends meet, would have one less thing to worry about while he was battling cancer. He worked very hard to support our family when we were growing up, and didn't deserve this to happen to him. Since he didn't want me to go back home to be there for him, I was hoping to help him in an indirect way.

I had rented a second floor studio apartment downtown. It had a balcony with an ocean view, and was about 3 blocks from the Pacific ocean. The rent was 2,300 pesos, or $230.00 US per month. There wasn't a lot to it, a bed, bathroom with shower, and miniature fridge. But it was great! Just living in the city, and interacting with indigenous people was quite an experience. I started working at the Villa del Palmar, a resort where I had stayed before. A three star resort, but nothing like the Bay View Grand. Like all the other resorts in the area it took quite a pounding from Kenna. The first and second floor bungalow's were ravished by Kenna's force. Once again a terrible sight to see. I would take the bus to and from work each day, high on weed of course, for about 3 pesos each way, or $.60 round trip. The buses in Vallarta were old school buses that were painted white. It was always and adventure taking the bus. Speeding down the road to your destination, as you're bouncing up and down, then abruptly stopping at the different bus stops to unload and re-load hard working souls. It's amazing there aren't more accidents in Vallarta. I mean, if it were a city in the states there would be numerous crashes a day. But in Mexico, one needs to be more careful, or the Federales would get involved. A word that sends shivers down the spine of both tourists, and Mexican citizens alike.

Working at a resort trying to sell a timeshare after a category 5 hurricane wasn't the best idea in hindsight, but I had to give it a shot. There were fewer tourists, and more liner's since some resorts had closed down do to structural damage. A liner is someone who takes you on the timeshare tour and presentation. I tried for a couple of weeks, getting close a couple of times, but was ultimately let go because of the ratio of liner's to tourists. I decided to enjoy my last couple of weeks in Vallarta before returning to Phoenix, and start looking for a teaching position at mid year. While working at the Villa Del Palmar I met another liner by the name of Cory, who was originally from Canada. It's amazing the number of Americans and Canadians that actually live in Vallarta. Well, Cory and I made a good pair, he knew where to get the drugs, and I wanted to party like a MOFO, since I felt like I let my dad down again.

Chapter 4

The First Time

The last two weeks in Vallarta started out like most of my time there in the past. There was plenty of marijuana and cocaine, not to mention the alcohol consumed. For the first week we probably averaged about an 8 ball of coke and a quarter ounce of weed a day. You could say, basically, a non-stop ride in the fast lane, living la vida loca. We were getting out of control, walking the streets of Vallarta from time to time acting abhorrent. Cory was fluent in Spanish, because he lived there since he was a kid, so he would speak belligerently to the people as we walked the streets looking for women and trouble. We almost got into a couple of fights which isn't a good idea anywhere, but especially in Mexico. If the Federales catch you, they will lock you up and throw away the key, not to mention all the drugs we were doing and had in our possession.

We got our drugs from one of Cory's acquaintances, Sergio, an axiomatic member of one of the Cartel's according to Cory. Cory would give him a call on the pay phone outside, and he would show up with what we wanted. On one of his deliveries, Sergio dropped off a freebie of this beige colored drug that we soon learned was crack-cocaine. I had dibble-dabbled with the stuff in the past, just enough to get a voracious appetite for it. It was an appetite acquired in El Paso when I used to freebase cocaine wasting more coke than creating the crack-like substance obtained from the process. So, when this arrived it was like I said to myself, "Yes, finally I have a good amount to try!" I was hoping that the cravings that I had for so long would finally be satisfied, but in reality it just made my desire for the hard drug that much greater.

The last week in Mexico I became more paranoid and isolated. We rarely went out, only to get more beer, tequila, and something to eat, if anything at all. I just had to keep smoking crack and snorting cocaine. I just couldn't get enough. Clubbing for babes turned into flagging down taxis from the balcony to get us some hookers. Instead of one 8 ball now it was becoming close to two a day. Acting belligerent and defiant from the balcony to the Federales driving by on the road below, I'm surprised we didn't end up in a Mexican jail. We walked the line just enough to be major assholes, however, I could tell they were hoping that we would cross that line, so they could do their job.

It was a good thing the stay came to an end when it did, because I surely would have gotten into trouble or died. Leaving gave me a false sense of control over crack-cocaine. I didn't know where to get it back in Phoenix, so I had to stop. The hunger, although, stayed the same for this powerful, hard drug. In the back of my mind, I still had the convoluted hope, that once again, some day I would encounter this controlling drug that I thought I controlled, and oh boy, did I get my wish.

Chapter 5

Reunited With Ophelia

I arrived back in Phoenix in early December. It had been two months since I had seen Ophelia, which had been the longest time I had been away from her since her arrival in my life in 1993. I can remember walking into the house and seeing her white, little, fuzzy face surrounded by patches of black, brown, and orange trotting towards me. I picked her up and gave her a big old kiss. She probably thought I was trying to squash her, as I hugged her like a bear. Ophelia was a special felis catus. Her many talents included fetching rubber bands, rolling when directed, and answering back when spoken to. Her "Meow" would change with the question asked and the mood she was in. She was my little girl. It seemed as if there was a little person in there. To this very day, when I think about her fetching, rolling, and speaking it brings a smile to my eye, and a tear rolling down my cheek. Ophelia died in the spring of 2007, but would have lived longer if it were not for my drug use. My addiction to drugs, both soft and hard, was so strong that not even my love for her could penetrate it.

Ophelia stayed with a friend, and former colleague of mine while I was in Vallarta. When I arrived back in Phoenix, Ray let Ophelia and I stay with his family and him while I looked for a mid-year teaching position. Ray is a good old soul. Another teacher dedicating his life to help children and society. That year there were no teaching positions at mid year, at least the districts I was concentrating on. Since there were no teaching jobs to speak of, I decided to give selling home security systems a try at a local home security firm for the month of January. I made enough money during the month, so I decided to get an apartment of my own. The apartment was at another seedy place in west Phoenix. Once again, not the best place to live, but the rent was cheap. Walking and knocking, going door to door 6 days a week wasn't my thing after all, so I decided to leave the home security system business after January. For the months of February and March I decided to take some time off, spend time with Ophelia, and keep in contact with my dad before I looked for a substitute teaching position for the last 2 months of the school year. My drug use continued, and once again the drugs used were marijuana and cocaine. There were a couple of crack-addicted prostitutes that would come around from time to time, but I never pursued the drug remembering the last two out of control weeks in Vallarta. I resisted the temptation for the time being.

I landed a substitute teaching job with the Mesa Public Schools for the last two months of the '02-'03 school year. The money wasn't great, but it was fun teaching at the elementary level especially after teaching at the middle school level for over fourteen years. Don't get me wrong, I love the middle school child and I got into teaching at that level because of my own struggles when I was in seventh grade, but it's a beast you can't understand unless you've experienced it. I really feel that everyone should teach a week at some level, then you'd understand the sacrifices teachers make for your children. You may think that teaching is easy, but it is one of the hardest things I've ever done. We teach for the love of the children, because it's certainly not for the money.

At the end of the school year Ophelia and I went back to Iowa for a month or so to spend time with my family, and it was my 20 year high school reunion. I didn't know where to get drugs in the metropolis known as Waukon, Iowa, so I took a quarter pound of weed with me for my own personal use. It was good seeing a lot of old friends that I hadn't seen for many years, but my drug use was still controlling me. No one knew I was smoking pot, because I kept it very well hidden. In college I wrote a paper about marijuana use and learned that one can adapt to smoking weed and everyday life. I got high when I woke up, and was high when I went to bed at night. Something I had been doing since 1989. It definitely wears you down, but not as much as using hard drugs like heroin, meth, cocaine and crack.

Ophelia and I left Iowa sometime in July, and on the way back when we had a close call with a tornado. I checked the forecast the night before we left, and like many summer days in the mid-west there was a chance for severe weather the following day. The drive through Iowa and Nebraska was uneventful, so I figured there was no chance to see a tornado which is a phenomena I've been fascinated with since I had been a child. Well, as we left Nebraska, and traveled into Colorado on I-76 the clouds were becoming more dark. As we passed Sterling, CO the clouds were quite ominous rolling off the rocky mountains, and it turns out that what I was looking at was a horizontal funnel cloud. Before I knew it, it was black as night, even though it was only mid afternoon. There was grass and dirt flying through the air as we continued down the interstate. I could feel the force of the tornado pulling the truck, and then realized we were only going about 35 mph even though I had the pedal to the metal. I was thinking about pulling over, and getting me and Ophelia in the ditch next to the road, but then I saw a, "Next exit ½ mile" sign. We made it to the exit. I was going to pull under the over pass, but it was filled with cars, so I took a little dirt road to a convenience store that was full of gas pumps and propane tanks. As I was turning the truck around to position us in a better spot to leave if things got worse, I saw what looked to be a F-5 tornado rolling across the field on the other side of the interstate. It was a huge black monster and luckily is was approximately 5 miles away from us. After the tornado lifted I decided to hit the road again since we were parked in a dangerous area. We took off, and after 15 minutes or so of erratic, frantic driving the west end of the front passed, and the sun brightened the skies.

After spending a couple of days in the beautiful Colorado wilderness, Ophelia and I made it back to Phoenix. Ray was kind enough to put us up again for a week or so as I looked for a teaching position for the '03-'04 school year. I received calls from different districts, but was holding out for Mesa Public Schools. I got the call in mid-July from MPS, and turned out that they had numerous math openings at different schools, but I ultimately settled on teaching eighth grade math at Shepherd Junior High. I had always wanted to teach in the district, something about teaching in one of the largest districts in Arizona, and the pay would be a bit more. Up to this point I had taught in districts that had middle schools, and utilized the middle-school philosophy, but MPS had junior high schools. Junior highs are a bit like small high school factories, so I knew it would be an adjustment, but was willing to give it a shot. A little more money is huge for a teacher, especially when that teacher is an addict.

My appetite for cocaine dwindled because I had done so much in the past. I would do so much that my nose would bleed, but would just keep on snorting the drug. Just the smell of cocaine made me sick. I can't tell you how many times I thought I was going to drop dead as my heart would pound and couldn't catch my breath. I was still smoking marijuana everyday, despite that fact that first year at Shepherd JH was a successful one. My test scores were solid and I coached the 9th grade boys tennis team to a city championship. It was the first boys tennis championship in school history so that was really cool to be a part of. Those kids were really talented, and if we wouldn't have won the championship it would've been a disappointing year. Those kids hold a special place in my heart to this day, and I hope they are doing well and drug free. The banner that we won, and the banner that I won't ever see again, is hanging from the rafters in the gym. The reason I won't ever see it again is that I've been banned from MPS property for life because of what happened the next year. Just another thing that drug addiction has deprived me of.

The school year ended the last week of May, so for the month of June I headed back down to Puerto Vallarta. Me and my addiction to crack-cocaine were hoping to find Cory, so we could continue what we had started back in '02. After looking a few days for him I had no luck, just a few people said that they may have seen him here or there. Since Cory wasn't available I had to get the drugs I craved to feed my addiction from my old sources. One night when I was hanging out at the Zoo bar I met a couple of real good people. His name was Manny and her name was Dawn. They were closers at a resort in Nuevo Vallarta, a tourist area about 10 miles north of Puerto Vallarta. A closer is someone that finalizes the timeshare deal. They were transplanted Canadians, and they liked to party.

We hung out the last couple of weeks, and there was plenty of coke and smoke. Even though the smell of cocaine made me sick I still did it because I was an addict, it was available, and crack-cocaine wasn't. It was also the first time that I did ecstasy. I have to say I liked it, and it apparently has a bit of heroin in it, so I can see how it would be very addicting and has destroyed many lives. Heroin and ecstasy were two drugs that weren't available to me during my drug years, or I would have become addicted to that as well. I know heroin would've been the end of me after hearing some of the horror stories about heroin. Manny wanted me to stay down there and work at the timeshare, but ironically I didn't want to keep doing cocaine. Since I was under contract to teach for MPS for the '04-'05 school year, ultimately I went back to Mesa. That's when my personal addiction-from-hell story erupted.

Chapter 6

The Beginning Of The End

I arrived back in Mesa the first week of July, and moved into the hotel turned into apartments as I said earlier. It turns out it was the worst decision of my life. I started moving my things into the apartment one warm Mesa evening, and that's when I met the devil himself who went by the name of Jerry. Jerry was a crack-head that preyed on other peoples addiction to fuel his own. I can remember seeing him leaning up against the balcony of the second floor and telling myself that this guy looks like trouble. It turns out he was. As I was carrying a load up to the apartment, he acknowledged me and I him. You know, small talk like, "Hey, how are you?" "Good, how about you?" Stuff like that. Jerry was a likeable guy, he had the gift of gab. Now, I realize he was just after someone to buy him drugs. Me and my addiction to crack-cocaine were his meal ticket. After moving all my stuff into the apartment, I bought some beer and invited my next door neighbor over for a cold one. Of course, Ophelia came trotting out to show off for the new guest. He, like all others that met this fuzzy little feline, was captivated and charmed. She wooed even those that didn't like cats. She went right over to Jerry and started rubbing against his legs walking back and forth in front of him. Ophelia would always meander over to a guest like this bringing a smile to their faces, Jerry was quite amazed that a precious, little, delicate creature like Ophelia could show him affection. Probably something to do with growing up in the environment he did. As it turned out he was an ex-gang member from Los Angeles. I know cats behave this way to transfer their scent on to someone for familiarity, but the way Ophelia lit up a room I believe there was more to it than that. It was then that Jerry uttered those infamous words as he said, "Could I borrow some money to get some medicine?" I knew it must be for some illegal drug, and it turned out to be for crack-cocaine. I gave him the money on the condition I could have some too. Turned out to be another terrible choice.

Sitting on pins and needles for an hour or two, he finally came back with the hard drug that I craved since becoming addicted in '02 when I lived in Puerto Vallarta. To smoke crack we used an empty beer can in Puerto Vallarta, because we didn't know how to use and where to get a glass pipe. We were way to paranoid to go look for one anyway. This was the first time I smoked crack from a glass pipe. It was a much purer hit and therefore much more powerful than I had experienced in the past. It took my addiction to a new level, and I immediately was asking for more. It was just what Jerry was hoping for, because when we finished what he had gotten I drove him back to the place where he had gotten the first rock. The place we drove to was in west Mesa to one of the little sleazy motels on Main

Street that was even more enfeebled than the Apartments where I lived. Jerry directed me where to go, we pulled up to the room, he got out, and I waited for him in the truck. There is nothing more nerve racking than waiting outside a "Crack house" for an illegal hard drug when there are police cruising by. I knew it was wrong and foolish, but when you're addicted it just doesn't matter. Apathy makes consequences a mute point.

This was going to be a one night thing with this hard drug, but my addiction and Jerry had different thoughts. There was still a month until the school year was going to start, so I felt like there was no harm. I was wrong. When I woke the next morning, which was probably the last good night of sleep I had the next 8 months, my addiction was wanting more crack-cocaine. I told myself that as long as I quit before the start of school it would be alright, so I knocked on Jerry's door and we were off to score some more crack. By the time the month of July had passed the $20 rock had progressed to a gram which was $40. My addiction was full blown even though I didn't want to believe it. I just kept telling myself that I was going to get tired of it and that I was going to stop. Sleep was becoming a rare commodity, because I couldn't stop smoking the hard drug. I started losing weight since I was eating less, or not at all some days. The tan that I brought back from Vallarta was turning pale.

August was here, so I knew I had to stop smoking since school was about to start. I had a terrible habit since I had been smoking crack-cocaine every day for a month, so I knew I had to stop for at least 23 days to form a good habit, but I couldn't. That was something easier said than done being addicted to a hard drug, and having a crack head living next door. Needless to say, instead of quitting my addiction kept progressing, and I was losing control.

The first week of school was set to start the first week of August. The first five days consisted of boring meetings, going over strategies and concepts that were already learned previous years. Not a practical use of time like getting the classroom ready for the upcoming year. That was usually something that would have to be done on our own time. It was always difficult getting back into the swing of things after summer vacation, but starting the year a slave to a crack-cocaine addiction was extremely difficult. The five days of meetings were usually separated by the weekend, so I was hoping I would be able to end the crack-cocaine use by the time the kids started. Thursday and Friday were usually slower to ease the teachers back into the school year. When the meetings ended I would come up with an excuse to leave early, or just slip out the back to speed home to feed my addiction to this horrific hard drug.

It was the last weekend before school started with the kids on Thursday. Instead of quitting, I gave into my addiction to crack, and went on a binge hoping to quench my crack addiction. This only pushed me farther into addiction. Jerry and I probably smoked at least an eight ball that weekend which is about 3 grams. Hardly getting any sleep from the binge, Monday morning came way too soon and it was time for another three days of meetings. Reality was starting to set in, and in four days the kids were going to be back. I was addicted to crack-cocaine.

Smoking probably a gram a night, and not getting much sleep the next three nights, I started the year off with the kids pretty much exhausted. The first two days with the students went OK, since it consisted of learning class rules, schedules, filling out paper work, etc. When the end of the day came around on Friday, I couldn't get out of there fast enough to go feed my addiction. That weekend we smoked about an eight ball again, and maybe slept four hours over the weekend. I tried to shield Ophelia from the terrible second hand smoke by keeping her in the bedroom. But she wanted to be with me so I would let her out new and then. I could tell the smoke was affecting her because she would cough and her eyes were glossy, but I couldn't stop. I would tell myself that I was killing her, but it didn't matter. That is how powerfully evil drug addiction is.

Since I didn't sleep Sunday night, I took a sick day on Monday. It was only the third day of classes and something I hadn't done my previous 15 years in the profession. Tennis would be starting soon, so I knew I wouldn't be able to take off much more time. However, the madness continued, and we smoked another gram on Monday. Somehow I made it to work on Tuesday, and when I arrived at school I made up a excuse about being sick. People believed me because they had no reason not to. The secretary in the office asked me if I was losing weight, because I looked a little skinny. I had always worked out and lifted weights throughout my life, but when I became addicted to the hard drug, crack-cocaine, that stopped. Smoking at least a gram of crack a night, hardly getting any sleep, and then teaching Junior High math wasn't easy. The crack-cocaine addiction was slowly killing me, but being a professional I knew I had a job to do, so I did the best I could.

By the time September came I was even deeper into the addiction. I was starting to get worried, because I was getting the feeling that I couldn't stop. In mid September the Iowa Hawkeye football team had a game against the Arizona State Sun Devil's. Growing up in Iowa, I am a huge Hawkeye fan, GO HAWKS! The Friday before the game the I-club was holding a rally at a sports bar in Tempe. I was supposed to meet my best friend of close to thirty years there to celebrate the Hawk's at the pep rally. Jim and I grew up in Waukon, Iowa, a small town in northeast Iowa. Having only sisters, Jim is the closest thing that I will have to a brother. Growing up we would hang out and do what friends do in a small town. Things like throw around the football, go fishing, cruise around town on the moped, etc. We were also roommates at the University of Northern Iowa, GO PANTHERS! There is only one thing that would make me stand-up my life-long friend, a crack-cocaine addiction. I felt terrible, but I couldn't tear myself away from that stuff.

We stayed up all night once again smoking, and the Hawks had a game on Saturday. Jim had no idea that I was addicted to crack-cocaine, because I was still able to hide it at this point. To tell you the truth, I still didn't think I was addicted either, because I was in denial. The I-club was holding a pregame party on Saturday afternoon at another Tempe establishment. Jim picked me up at 1pm, and we were off to get ready for the Hawks. It wasn't easy leaving the crack pipe, but the Hawks were in town. To counteract the crack high, and deal with not being able to smoke for a while, I started drinking heavily at the event. By the time the game started I was quite intoxicated. We had "Nose bleed" seats in the Iowa section at Sun Devil Stadium. The game didn't go well for the Hawks, and I became quite belligerent. I don't remember what the score was in the second quarter, but the game was a blow out. I was yelling obscenities about the Hawks because we were getting trounced. The section of Hawkeye fans didn't appreciate this, so we were kicked out of the game. Pretty embarrassing, but I was actually glad because I wanted to smoke more crack. How terribly sad is that?!

September ended the way it had started, constantly smoking crack-cocaine, hardly eating, and not sleeping for days at a time. By this time I was really getting worried, because I started to realize I wasn't going to be able to stop. Realizing I didn't have control of something that I thought I did was pretty scary. I didn't seek help because I was ashamed and didn't want to burden anyone with my problem. I got myself into this, so I was going to get myself out of this addiction. I knew my teaching was suffering, and I felt bad about that, but I tried to do the best I could living in a horrific addiction.

Chapter 7

Losing Control

When October arrived I had more time on my hands because tennis was finishing up. I was able to leave school at 4pm now compared to 5:30pm when I was coaching. I would smoke for longer amounts of time, so I was smoking more crack-cocaine. My addiction went to yet another level. At this point, I was spending 60% or more of my pay-check each month on crack. For the next two weeks I slept maybe twelve hours the whole time. I had been telling myself the last three months that I would get bored with the hard drug and quit. I couldn't! Again, when you feel like you're in control, and then realize you're not it is quite horrifying. Anyone who thinks they can control drug use is a fool, and only kidding themselves. That is exactly what I was; a fool.

In mid October we had a fall break. Jim and I had scheduled a trip to Las Vegas like we did each fall. I was supposed to leave Thursday morning, and return on Sunday night. Jim was going to meet me there Saturday morning, and return on Monday morning.

Wednesday was an early release day for the students. Staff was supposed to stay until 4pm, but I skipped out early. When I got home Jerry and I immediately cruised back to the crack house for another gram. After another night of non-stop crack smoking, I missed my flight Thursday to continue the sickness. We smoked all day and Thursday night as well, not sleeping a wink, but somehow made it to the airport on Friday morning a couple of hours before the flight left.

When I finally made it through security, I had to find a bar to start drinking to counteract the withdrawals. When I sat down, I immediately got a large draft beer and a shot of tequila. Sitting next to me at the bar was a gorgeous blond woman from Reno, Nevada. We hit it off right away and started talking, and turned out she was on the same flight as me. The topic of drug use came up at some point in the conversation. She told me she was originally from California, but moved away because she got addicted to crack-cocaine also. We sat together during the flight to Las Vegas and enjoyed each others company. I tried to convince her to stay the night with me in Vegas, but she had to get back to Reno for business. After I checked into the casino I slept the whole night anyway because I was so exhausted from three months of smoking crack non-stop.

The trip was a bit of a drag, because I was pretty much out of it. Instead of having a great time like always in Vegas, I was constantly thinking about smoking crack. When I got back to the apartment Sunday night, I immediately knocked on Jerry's door then we went to get another gram. Once again we were up all night smoking, and then it was time for school Monday morning. I kept telling myself,

"Only five more weeks before Thanksgiving break, and that I could make it." I slept a total of about thirty hours the next five weeks, and my teaching was really starting to suffer. The students were acting up and parents were starting to call with complaints. The principal and head of the math department had a meeting with me discussing the complaints, but I played it off saying the kids were difficult this year and I would get it together.

Finally, Thanksgiving arrived and not a minute too soon. My body was becoming run down due to the constant crack smoking, and not sleeping. I was five months into a crack addiction where I averaged six to ten hours of sleep a week, not to mention teaching junior high math. Some friends were starting to notice that I was losing weight, and some questioned if I was using. I denied anything was wrong. The shame you feel during an addiction is overwhelming. I didn't want to burden anyone with my problem. I had gotten myself into this mess, and would get myself out of it or die trying. Even though I didn't want to keep using my addiction progressed to two grams a day.

I don't think I slept the entire break. I could tell that Ophelia was being affected more and more. At times I would wipe tears from her eyes as I would weep myself. I was killing this special little fuzz ball who was constantly at my side, and who I loved like a daughter. My biggest fear was dying, and leaving her alone in the world. The disease of addiction could give a rats ass about love, because its main focus is misery and death.

As December arrived I knew I was in trouble. Not fully understanding addiction, I didn't understand why I couldn't stop smoking the hard drug. The despair I felt from the addiction was utterly terrible. I felt like I was probably going to end up dying from my drug use at this time. Even though I felt this way I didn't ask for help because I thought it was a sign of weakness, but now I know asking for help is a sign of strength. My niece's birthday is on December 3rd, so feeling like each day could have been my last I called her the night before to wish her a happy birthday. My sister thought this was so kind, but in reality I called because I didn't know if I'd be alive the next day to call her. In mid December I also got in touch with a former girlfriend in El Paso. She informed me that we had won a judgment in lawsuit against West Texas Mortgage for a real estate deal that had gone bad. Because I had lost touch with her due to my addiction to drugs, the judgment was lost. This news drove me deeper into my addiction, and the apathy I felt grew stronger. I just felt like dying.

Finally, after smoking crack non-stop the first three weeks of December, Christmas break arrived. In my mind I wanted to sleep and end the strangle hold that the crack addiction had on me, but that didn't happen. We just kept on smoking and drinking. I had been asking the Good Lord to please help me stop for some time now, and he was starting to give me signs that trouble was near. For instance, the first weekend of break, Jerry and I went to the area where we were getting the crack to score some more of the terrible hard drug. Jerry entered the place and came back empty handed. He said his connection told him the area was hot, and there were rumors that a bust was going to occur. We left the complex and went across the street to a fast food restaurant parking lot to check things out. Well, sure enough about ten minutes later a swarm of undercover police vehicles sped in and raided the place. It was like an episode of "The Shield". Five or six vehicles speeding up to the joint, undercover police jumping out with vests on and guns drawn. It was really quite surreal. I had been smoking crack for six months non-stop, so I was in a daze not believing what I was seeing. That was the first real sign from God to quit or else. But, I was so deep into the addiction, all I wanted to do was keep on smoking the crap.

Since the usual place that we got our crack from was shut down, we had to find a new place to get our drugs. Jerry got in contact with an old connection. His name was Louis and he had been living in the same area as his former dealer. The new location was an "Extended stay" type hotel in west Mesa, close to Tempe. Getting tired of supporting Jerry's habit, and it being a much safer location than the other area, I started to make the trip on my own. The addiction had progressed to at least two grams of crack a day at this point, and just when I didn't think it could get any worse I got a phone call from home. On the phone was my mother, and from the tone of her voice I knew it was bad news. My cousin Tommy, a great young man, had just graduated from college. He was attending a Christmas party in Rochester, MN and apparently one of his friends needed to get back to St. Paul where they lived. It was late at night, the weather wasn't the best being mid December in Minnesota, and they hit some black ice. The car went off the road, rolled, and he was ejected and killed. I couldn't believe what I was hearing! Here I was addicted to crack-cocaine, and felt if anyone deserved to die it was me. I was floored and fell deeper into addiction. I felt responsible in a way, and my will to live was diminishing.

Addiction makes one very selfish, and that is why I ultimately started going over to Louis' on my own, so I could have all the crack to myself. It didn't take long for Louis to start taking advantage of me also. For instance I would pay for an 8-ball, but get a gram or less instead. I knew I was getting ripped off, but was so addicted I didn't care. The heat must have been getting to Louis because he had to move again. This time to Tempe. I started buying less from him since he was giving me less. Addiction makes no sense, because even though I was spending close to $2000.00 a month on crack, I was tired of getting ripped off.

On January 1st the Hawkeyes were playing LSU in the Capital One Bowl. Jim had invited me over to his place to watch the game, something that we always did. Christmas break was coming to an end and I'm not sure if I had slept even ten hours leading up to game time. Kick-off was at 11:30. I struggled to make it on time because I had smoked all night and morning leading up to the game. At half-time I made an excuse to drive home so I could smoke a bit more. By the time I made it back the second half had already begun. During the second half is when I started slipping in and out of consciousness. It was a great game that ended on a last second pass for a touchdown and Hawkeye victory, and I just about missed it. Instead of staying to finish a great day of football with Jim and his family like usual, I made an excuse and bolted to continue my smoking of crack-cocaine.

Chapter 8

From Eminent Death To Life

January 3rd was the first day of the second semester. I was exhausted from a six month crack addiction, and just ended a two and a half week break where I had slept just a handful of hours. I literally had one foot in the grave. To make things worse, I was informed that two of my best classes were going to be taken away from me and I was going to inherit two classes with unruly students. Many of the students had behavior problems. To deal with the stress, I started leaving during my breaks to smoke more crack. I was spinning out of control.

One day after school, I called Louis to score another gram, but his phone was disconnected. I went to the Tempe apartment anyway to see if he was there. The other times I had gone over there I noticed a couple of shady characters hanging around. They were there once again, and when there was no answer at Louis' apartment, I asked them if they knew where to get some crack. They went into one of the apartments, and after a couple of minutes they came back out to invite me in. They introduced me to a young woman who went by the name of "Giggles". She asked me what I was looking for, and I replied, "Crack-cocaine." She gave an actual gram for $40.00, so I was quite happy. That was the beginning of the end.

The rest of January I was spinning more and more out of control. Constant smoking before, during, and after school, while getting no sleep at night. It was becoming apparent that something was wrong and people were starting to notice. A friend of mine, Todd, was questioning me if I was using, but the addiction was so strong I just denied it. He and his girlfriend Kelly would invite me over to grill out or what not. If I made it over it was always a couple of hours later than we had planned. The crack pipe wouldn't let me leave.

By the time February came around I wasn't in good shape. I was so exhausted from a seven month crack addiction I was even starting to fall asleep at school. Jim and I went to the Phoenix Open golf tournament as we did each year. As we were sitting by one of the greens I actually passed out because I was so exhausted. Also, I was extremely hungry because I wasn't eating well. One doesn't have much of an appetite when you're addicted to crack-cocaine, or other hard drugs for that matter. At the tournament I got a hot dog, and I can remember gobbling it down. I think it was the first thing I ate in two days. I could tell Jim was taken aback a bit, but I just lied, and said everything was alright. The next day was the Super Bowl which fell on February 6th that year. I went over to a friends house for a SB party. Three other friends of mine, Mike, Chrissy, and Julie organized a bit of a surprise birthday party for me since I was turning 40 on February 7th. It was really cool of them to think of me and make that day special. Whoever first said that life begins at 40 was a very wise person.

I ended up taking Monday off from school since it was my birthday. It was really just another excuse to waste another day and keep smoking crack. At SJH they have a cake for you on your birthday, and by not showing up, displaying all the erratic behavior that I had been displaying, the principal put me under investigation. The last three weeks of February were a nightmare. I'm not sure if I slept at all. I was constantly smoking, not eating, and not sleeping. I came close to passing out in front of the students when I would be doing problems for them at the overhead projector. One day after school when I was speeding home, I almost didn't notice a line of cars at a red light. I noticed the cars at the last second and slammed on the breaks stopping just in time. Thank God because I would have killed someone for sure. At night I would beg God to help me stop. I could tell Ophelia was becoming more ill as well from the second hand smoke. It was horrifying.

I was receiving numerous and increasing signs from the Good Lord, but was too far gone to care. My behavior was becoming more and more disturbing as well. The police had my apartment under surveillance, although I didn't realize it or want to believe it at the time. I lived on the second floor, and the cops would congregate in the back parking lot under my window. I would blow the smoke out of the window to try to keep it from Ophelia. There were times that there would be a flash because I think they were trying to photograph me. I'd dress all in black like a ninja to try to make it hard for them to see me. The addiction was driving me insane, because it seemed like a game to me. One minute weeping and begging God to help me stop, and the next minute taking another hit blowing smoke out the window slowly killing myself and Ophelia. One night I drove to the convenience store down the road to get some beer to counteract the crack high, and a cop pulled me over. I hadn't been drinking yet so there was no alcohol on my breath, so he let me go after a quick sobriety test. If that wasn't a sign I don't know what was, but I had accepted the fact that it was my time to die. I had given up all hope. That is what addiction does, it takes all hope away from its victims.

After school on February 28th I rushed to Giggles house and scored a couple of grams. I was up all night smoking once again, and ran out at about 5am on March 1st. I had to leave for school in a couple of hours, and I was out of crack. I spent the next couple of hours scraping used pipes because I was having major withdrawals. I drug myself to school, got through my first period class, and then hit the road for Giggles place when class was over around 10:00am. I got to her place at about 10:10am, and walked into the house. Quickly, I bought a gram and left.

As I was walking out the door to my truck I noticed a helicopter hovering overhead. I asked myself if that was because of me, but shrugged it off and hit the road for my apartment. I sped home since I didn't have a lot of time before the next class started. I was feeling a bit nervous because of the helicopter that I had noticed. I checked the mirrors to see if anyone was following me, but didn't notice anyone behind me, so I thought everything was OK. As I pulled up to the apartments I noticed a police cruiser in front of me. I stopped to let him by me, but he motioned for me to pull in. I pulled into the parking lot and that's when he turned on the cherries. Then an unmarked car came zooming into the lot, and I knew it was over. I parked the truck, got out, and waited for the undercover officers to come over and make the arrest. As I waited at least another six unmarked cars pulled up. I had time to get rid of the crack, or make a run for it, but was just thankful it was over. When they finally came over I told them it was in my pocket. After the undercover cop got the gram he said, "You know this is ours, don't you?" I replied. "I'm just glad it's over." I truly believe I would've been dead by the end of the month if I hadn't been arrested. They saved my life.

I checked myself into rehab about a week later at Banner Health Rehabilitation Center, and lived at twelve step program meetings for the next four months. They kept me clean and gave me hope. In mid summer I took a plea deal which resulted in a year and a half of probation. It wasn't easy, but after about twelve months of serving probation, I was discharged for successfully completing the program.

You don't want your children to become addicted to drugs as I did, it is horrible. I want all children out there to understand that doing drugs is utterly wrong and not cool. Drugs are evil, and only send you down a road to nowhere. Drugs kill, if they don't kill you they will kill your dreams. Yes, I survived my addiction, but I've done a lot of damage to my body, and I know my life will be cut short from all my past drug use.

If you are using drugs, you may think that you aren't addicted, but you could become addicted if you aren't already. Ask for help before it's too late, and your hopes and dreams are no more! You will find strength in asking for help. The only one you are fooling is yourself. Don't be a fool and follow in my footsteps! Also, if you know of a family member that is struggling with drug addiction have the courage to get them help, because they absolutely need your love and support, and they will thank you in the long run. The drug addictions that I went through were the most horrifically terrifying, and despair filled occurrences I've ever gone through, and is something I wouldn't wish on anyone. You are loved so much, and have too much love to give to waste your life on drugs. It took me many years, but I have accepted God's forgiveness for my sins, hence I have forgiven myself for my sins. God's love has truly saved me, and God's love will save you as well.

.

Edwards Brothers Malloy
Thorofare, NJ USA
May 10, 2013